I AM

Vision Book

From Religious Rules
to Metaphysical Principles

PAUL CAMPBELL, METAPHYSICIAN

BALBOA.
PRESS

A DIVISION OF HAY HOUSE

Balboa Press books may be ordered through booksellers or by contacting:

Balboa Press
A Division of Hay House
1663 Liberty Drive
Bloomington, IN 47403
www.balboapress.com
1 (877) 407-4847

Printed in the United States of America.

ISBN: 978-1-4525-9613-6 (sc)
ISBN: 978-1-4525-9614-3 (e)

Balboa Press rev. date: 04/23/2014

Contents

Thank you

To my parents for their love of God

To my many Spiritual Teachers in Atlanta,
Especially
The Rev. Dr. Joyce Rennolds

To Gloria Novak fellow musician
And Editor
For taking my Pennsylvania Dutch and
Pittsburghese and making
English sense

For the understanding
That being repelled is an
Indicator from
God/Universe
To shift my thinking

I AM
Vision Book

I talk about my 40 years in the desert
My transformation from Religious
Rules to Metaphysical Principles
How I apply these principles
Thought, Word and Action
Law of Attraction + Law of Repelling –
Owning my "I AM" my gifts
My understanding and interdependence
with God/Universe
How my light came to shine

This book contains space for you
to start your transformation
Suggestions to guide you
In understanding your God given
Vision and Dreams, and
How to Manifest and own your "I AM"

My Prayer

Source of all Good, God of the Universe,
Our Temple honors the God that lives in us.

We Flourish on Earth and fulfill your will,
We accept the entire Splendor
the Universe has for us.

As the Bird of the air and
the Lily of the Field,
We trust you Daily.

We forgive to create our Peace of Mind,
We say kind words to create Peace in others.

The absence of Faith is Fear, which
creates Evil and Temptation,
We have faith in you Giver of the Universe.

You are the Source of all good,
You are the Power that flows through us,
You are the Everlasting Light
that shines in us,
Forever and ever, And So It Is.

Who AM I?

As a child growing up in a Fundamentalist Christian Family, the Bible and more importantly the interpretation of the Bible ruled our lives. I was taught of an Anthropomorphic God (the attributes of human shape to a God), that sat on high watching our every move and making conscious decisions on our worthiness to receive.

My Bible told me of Adam and Eve who were thrown out of the Garden of Eden for not obeying God. Noah was told to build an Ark to save his family while God flooded the earth killing most of his creation. Lot was told to leave Sodom and Gomorrah so God could destroy with fire more of his creation, (God, a God of his word could not flood the earth again, the rainbow is a covenant not to kill with water again). Moses totally frustrated by The Children of Israel's whining for one-more-thing, struck the rock to make water flow instead of speaking to the rock as God told him to do; Moses frustration got him punished and he would not be permitted to go into the Promise Land. This is a God to be feared and my Mother knew how to use that fear in her favor.

Contrast my childhood understanding of the Genesis Story; "We are created in the image of God" with that of the Torah. "The Torah: A Modern Commentary, GE W. Gunther Plant. Genesis 1:27:

"So God Created the human being in (the divine) image, creating (them) in the image of God. . ."

This is Music to my ears and heart when I read "the divine image"; this is different from what I was taught as a child but is what I now believe; that:

I AM not a human being trying to be spiritual.

I AM "The Divine" in a human body.

I believe that there is only "ONE" God of the Universe, not different Gods, but that there are different understandings of Who and What this God is. "I" needed a new thought about God, "I" needed a new perception."

Fear ruled my life; if I made a mistake I would be shammed and punished. In my teen's I continued my expansion of studying music, playing in other churches and enrolled in a nearby Catholic College. The Pastor of my parents' church stood at the pulpit and pointed his finger at me and said in front of a full church that I would be nothing if I kept doing things outside of his church. He continued to say that God would not support me or bless me. God was used to control me, hence started my 40 years in the desert.

I did go to college, Conservatory and Graduate School, but in the back of my mind had guilt for wanting to be me and I was afraid to be me because of this God I Feared. I needed a new idea of God.

Why would God give me desires to accomplish and be creative in life and then have his Servants (Ministers) tell me I was wrong for wanting those thing in my heart, my dreams, My vision for who "I AM".

Jump ahead to the 21st century in the early 2000's; I was living in Atlanta and burnt out. I was introduced to Science of Mind, Metaphysics and many Gurus'. I learned of One Power, and Energy-Source that is called God of the universe. In Science of Mind we believe this God is everywhere, but when we are born God is made present on earth. As Jesus said. "We are the Temple of God" "We are God made Flesh".

This Energy Source, God of the Universe, does not think; it responds to our Thoughts and Direction. This God is always giving, loving and has NO recollection of our supposed wrong doings, only humans keep track of what they want to use to control us. This Energy Source God responds to our direction. We do not, as I did earlier in my life, beg and plead in prayer. We affirm the existence of what we are visioning and direct this energy source "God" to give us the opportunity to fulfill our vision.

God will and must respond to our thoughts and affirmations. This philosophy makes me more responsible than ever to be centered, calm, Living a Joyous and Happy life and the more we trust God, this God/Universe goes before me and sets-up situations for my success. My God/Universe goes before me and "Makes the path straight".

When I allow God/Universe to do what God does, God will and must respond to our thoughts and affirmations. Often we pre- determine how things are to be and we miss what is right in front of us. Let go and allow God to do what God does best and expand your thinking to see the good in everything in front of you as an action of God. We who study and practice Metaphysics own the "I AM" in us and say God will do one of three yes's:

1. Yes, NOW.
2. Yes, God is working out the details.
3. Yes, God is working out something better.

Be patient. This Energy Source, God/
Universe has NO time frame.
Have FUN. The more FUN you have doing this
The easier it will be to ALLOW.

In the years 2004 – 2012, I reinvented my life. I changed how I studied music, what I was thinking while practicing and what I was saying about my practice at the end of the day. I affirmed that "Yes that is so much better than yesterday's practicing". My performing changed, my teaching changed, everything changed because I was thinking something different and better.

I utilized the Spiritual Principles of "Thought, Word and Action" and the total belief that God/Universe was and is always responding to my Thoughts, Words and Action. I began to rebuild my performing in this period. I accepted Large Interim Positions as Organist, each interim position was between 5-8 months, when the interim was finished I moved on. I learned what I needed to learn and released what no longer worked for me and moved to the next position. I started to own ME, and the "I AM" within me.

My biggest Epiphany/Healing experience was about 2005. I was sitting in Satsung at Mahavatar Babigi Ashram, The Temple of the Inner Self with Guru Munishwarji Bayazid Walking Tall. That evening for our meditation Munishwarji had prepared little pieces of paper with a sentence on it (I don't remember what the sentence said). In our silent meditation we were to look at the first word, monitor our breathing and if nothing came to our mind we were to move to the next word until we got an intuitive hit. I believe it was with the third word that I remembered my Favorite Position in Pittsburgh as a Director of Music and Organist. I remembered that in the early ninety's a new pastor came to the church, we did not mesh and I was dismissed. I was unhappy and internalized the experience as unfair and became bitter.

When we were finished with our time meditating, Munishwarji as customary would ask people to talk about what came to mind. Being the good student and since no one else jumped to talk, I went first . . . I told where my mind had gone and that I had been fired.

In front of everyone, Munishwarji said: "So Paul, how long are you going to play the victim role?" This is where you want to smack your Guru and melt away, but you can't. I went home and out of respect for Munishwarji and myself I worked on forgiving, releasing and understanding what a gift this is now to move on. And I DID move on.

At the end of 2011 going into 2012, I noticed that jobs and teaching venues were drying up for me. I asked: "God, what's happening?" My Spiritual teachers said: "Paul, your energy is shutting down for you in Atlanta; God/Universe has something bigger for you". "Where are you being offered an opportunity"?

Things were getting tight financially and nothing seemed to be working for me other than my personal practicing and composing of music. In January of 2012 I was being inspired to compose another piano piece, a very hollow sounding arrangement on the tune "Be Still my Soul". After months of slowly composing I finished it around March.

A short time after finishing this section of "Be Still my Soul", I received a call from a friend. The friend said," Paul I have something to tell you. Mason, your best friend, was found at 5 AM on Tuesday morning in Piedmont Park. He was beaten and unconscious; He didn't make it." I said, "What do you mean He didn't make it?" He said, "We found him at the County Morgue".

My friend was gone . . . Be Still my Soul. I was crying WHY, WHY, WHY! For 5 years, Piedmont Park was our playground. This was where we walked, went swimming, laughed together, cried together or would just sit in silence. We met in Piedmont Park 5 years earlier on the Summer Solstice, June 22. We had a special spiritual connection with the Summer Solstice. This was because my Birthday is the Winter Solstice, December 22. Piedmont Park, our special playground, is where my friend left this plane. Mason and I had the most intimate relationship I had ever had, intimate but non-sexual.

My situation in Atlanta was not getting any better. I had an opportunity to stay with an old friend in Pittsburgh. When I left Pittsburgh in 1999, I sold my houses and swore I would never go back there.

In May of 2012, I was in the home of my friend Schelle Wilson (an Opera Singer) and her partners. I was in their kitchen making Apple Pie for them before I left Atlanta. Schelle's father Rev. Cicero Wilson was sitting there very calmly talking with me as I rolled pie dough. He said, "You are to leave Atlanta, you must go back to Pittsburgh" and then he looked at me and said:

"Joseph, you must go back to Egypt."

He said, "God has something for you in Pittsburgh, a person, a place or many opportunities. And remember, Joseph's enemies were made his footstools".

I escaped and left Pittsburgh a victim. I
returned solid in "Who I AM".
I hired movers, shipped my furniture and
on June 4th I drove back to Pittsburgh.
Pittsburgh was different; I was different.

Two days after arriving in Pittsburgh, some friends and I were in a public place and a man walked up and pointed at each of us; "No not you", "No not you", "Ah, it's you" he said. "I've been sent to cleanse your energy. May I touch your back?" I said yes. He did his cleansing and walked away, never to be seen again.

A few weeks after arriving in Pittsburgh I was settled enough to get back into my morning routine, Coffee, Meditation, Orange Juice, and Walk. Then around 9 AM

I'd start piano practicing. One morning the tune "Simple Gifts" popped into my head and a version of it emerged, in three different styles and keys: first "C" then "D flat" and "D". I went "WOW!" and then I remembered the words.

> I danced in the morning when the world was begun,
>
> I danced in the moon and the stars and sun,
>
> Dance, then. Wherever you may be,
>
> I am the Lord of the dance, Said He.
>
> And I'll lead you all, wherever you may be,
>
> And I'll lead you all in the Dance said He.

This was the other half of "Be Still my Soul". My friend Mason was dancing, dancing on the other side. In all it was the Sun, Moon and stars, the Solstice, our connection. What I didn't' tell you was that my friend Mason had said good bye to me several times . . . "Be Still my Soul" was for him. I didn't understand at the time until a few months later I was invited back to Atlanta to perform this piece at the "Cymatics Conference" at which many of Mason's friends attended the conference.

Months later I was at a party/event held by Heart of Pittsburgh where I met many people. I started to talk with a woman and after a few minutes she invited me to go with her the next night to a book reading of her new book "The Seer and The

Sayer". I said "yes" and offered to open her book reading by playing a half hour of piano music. She said "great".

Her name is Victoria Hanchin and that night I learned of her book "The Seer and The Sayer" and of her Journey, which is best found in a quote from her book; "This is what I have been summoned to do, I take my Divine Assignment Seriously".

Vikki, talks about Pittsburgh and the Mayan 2012 prophesies of the Mayan Calendar and the fourth river under Pittsburgh that begins in Ohio near the Maya Serpent Mound. I also learned about Pittsburgh and the Universal Portal and that this is a very strategic place to be when the Mayan Calendar ended December 21, 2012. The ending of this 26,000 year cycle was with a Planetary Alignment called the "Procession of the Equinox". Victoria Hanchin states in her book; "In all the hype of doom and mongering, many missed the lost message, that one can become a pathway to co-create a New Earth of unity and greater good".

The first day after the ending of the Mayan Calendar is December 22nd, My Birthday. In the days, weeks and months following, opportunities flowed and I continued to change and grow.

December 22, 2012 ended my 40 years in the desert and began my Divine Journey of the Promises of God/Universe.

This all sounds good. Understand that when I affirm change in my life and I believe it will happen, things start to MOVE. (We call it in Metaphysics a shift.) I came back to Pittsburgh with some furniture, a temporary place to stay and temporary jobs. When I want to move toward my vision of my life, things around me will move, some things leave, some things push me. I, in this period of my life, have had to say NO to so many people who want to suck me into their stuff or see my great energy and just want to use my energy. Becoming Spiritually Fit is knowing when to get involved and when not to get involved with people and their stuff. Most times I need to put my energy into "MY" projects, but I can verbally support other people's projects.

A spiritual Journey is called a Journey because I am moving, not getting attached, allowing things to come and go as they flow through my life. This is where I work the most, people who compare will say to me, "you're always doing different things", "Why don't you settle down?"; in other words become like them. I have a beautiful home, a place that is my safe place, a place to write, meditate, sleep and enjoy my life. But I'm already visioning the Creation/ Renovating of another house in my mind. Today I Manifest clothes, furniture, money, compose music, I perform in more and more places. I'm writing this book, finishing a second Children's book, recording piano music and speaking on a regular basis. With all that, if I want to achieve what I see for myself, more thoughts have to change (expand) to allow the growth.

Who AM I?
I AM an Infinite Possibility.
I AM a Manifestation of God.
I AM the divine.

Who do people say that I am?

This question is what Jesus asked when his disciples were questioning him; Jesus asked, "Who do people say that I am?"

I believe that Jesus didn't want to know what people were thinking about him. Jesus wanted to know what his disciple's perception was and what they were seeing and thinking, and/or had internalized.

The Kabala

Things are not as we see them,

Things are as we perceive them.

One hundred people can be in a room all observing the same event and one hundred people are going to have one hundred different stories about what they experienced.

There may be times to test the waters by listening or doing a survey for your business and/or your product. But when we act and do things out of "What people may think", we put more value on others opinion than on the vision we have for our life. The opinion of what you could do will continue to change as people decide how they want to control you.

Don't listen to people and have some discretion about your work until it's revealed to the public. Then people can see what you were working on. And don't listen to negative people; some people will always be jealous.

Listen to the voice of God/Universe that's inspiring your vision and then you will be successful.

Dr. Wayne D Dyer:

> "The greatest prison people live in is the fear of what people think."

Growing up in a Pentecostal Fundamentalist Church "I" was told "who I should be". Hmmm, as early as I can remember, I wanted to kiss the boys and not the girls. I was different and trying to be me and believing what a Pentecostal Fundamentalist Church was telling me was the beginning of my imprisonment. I tried to conform, but still wanted to play with my buddies and have a teenage boyfriend. I had a short marriage after college and then burst into my gay life. I was not very graceful at times; I had no role model to look to as I learned to be who "I" knew "I" was. I now owned all of who "I Am".

Today I work in many different denomination and traditions as Music Director/Pianist and Organist. It's what I love to do, move people with sound and the energy of God/Universe that flows through me.

In the 80's and 90's many mainline denominations in Pittsburgh were conducting witch hunts to find gay ministers and priests. Fear ran ramped, especially with friends who were either gay and or working in the church, or who were married and having a gay life on the side. I was openly gay and for the ministers who were hiding his/

her real identity I was not always popular with them. Many had to pretend and lie to their congregations, wives and themselves just to be Ministers in the church.

We were created in the (Image of God), but many were working for the church and being told by the church that what God created in us was wrong . . .

The Club/Bar seen was big. One night 20 plus years ago, I was out at Pegusus the bar on Liberty Ave. downtown Pittsburgh when a lover's quarrel broke out in the bar; a stabbing happened between these two lovers. The police locked down the bar with us all inside. I was more upset about the young man who was stabbed by his lover and died, But for the 5 ministers and priests that were there that night, panic struck. My friends, the ministers and priests said; "if TV crews come in and I'm caught here, I'm finished . . ."

Many who worked in the church bought into the belief of the church, so many lied about who they were. Many who work in the church resort to medicating on many levels, lying, alcohol, sex, drugs . . .

I have mourned the death of my former life in the church.

Today, "I AM" an independent Minister being
invited as Paul Campbell; Musician/Organist/
Pianist, Speaker and Metaphysician.
Who do people say that I am? A better question,
Who do "I" say that "I AM"?

I AM

"I AM" Paul Campbell. There is only one of me and there will never be another like me. I want to give you my understanding of where "I AM" originated and the evolution of "I AM" for me.

My first hearing of "I AM" was as a child in the Bible Story of God telling Moses to go to Egypt and tell the Pharaoh to let my people go. Moses resisted and said; "who shall I say sends me?" God said; say "I am that I am" has sent you. I have thought that the first "I AM" was for Moses and the second "I AM" was God---"I AM" Moses that the great "I AM" has sent. In the story, God is above and man is below, in Science of Mind we call this Duality, we are apart from each other, God reigns from above.

Joseph, "The Dreamer" told his older brothers of his dream that they would bow down before him one day. He was already the favorite of his father and disliked by his older brothers who despised his favor. His brothers threw him in a pit, ripped his clothes off and told their Father that an animal had killed his favorite son. Joseph was taken by a band of people to Egypt as a slave and ended up in prison. Joseph never abandoned his dreaming, even in prison word spread of his dreams and interpreting dreams. He was in and out of prison twice until the Pharaoh was having dreams and sent for Joseph, this man who could read dreams. Joseph interpreted the dreams, seven fat years, and seven lean years, Pharaoh made Joseph second in command under him to store up for the seven lean years. That is when Joseph sent for his brothers and family (there is more to the story) and Joseph's brothers bowed before Joseph not knowing that he was their youngest brother, the one they sold-out.

After a period of time, The Israelites were becoming too large in number and Pharaoh was becoming fearful, so he commanded the mid wives to kill at birth all males born to Hebrew women. Moses' Mother saved him and after three months she put him in a basket and floated him down the Nile in hope of him finding safety. Moses' Mother sent his sister Miriam to watch as he floated down the river. Pharaoh's daughter was bathing in the river and found Moses in the basket. Miriam watching all this said to Pharaohs daughter, "would you like me get a woman to nurse the baby for you?" Miriam got Moses' Mother. They were all brought into the Court/House of Pharaoh.

Moses learned both Egyptian customs from Pharaoh and his daughter and Hebrew customs from his Mother. One day Moses witnesses an Egyptian beating a Hebrew man and Moses Kill the Egyptian. The Pharaoh set out to find Moses and punish him; Moses ran into the mountains and went into hiding for years. "Sound Familiar?"

One day Moses was tending the sheep and he saw a bush with fire coming out of it, but the bush did not burn. Then the bush spoke to Moses. (It's also interesting to me that fire was used to talk to Moses; something that can consume or lighten.) God said; "Moses, Go to the Pharaoh and tell him to set my people free". Moses replied with all kinds of excuses until finally Moses said "who shall I say sends me?" God said "I am that I am sends you"; we know the story. Moses earlier in life was trained so he would have an understanding of the Court of Pharaoh; the very thing he is in hiding from. Moses is commanded to go back to Egypt, to "The Pharaoh". Moses was not put on this earth to watch sheep and stay in hiding, but to be who he could be; Moses, a leader, and he lead the Israelites out of Egypt. To become this Moses, Moses had to face his biggest fear.

There is another theory found in James Twyman's book called "The Moses Code". He presents a theory that's there's a missing comma. "I AM that I AM" needs a comma (,), "I AM that, I AM". When saying the word "that" it can refer to whatever you are seeing, or relating to, and that we are all One.

"Omkar" is a religious symbol of the Hindus. In the Beginning "Before the Beginning", The Brahman (absolute reality) was one and non-dual. It Thought, "I am one – may I become many". This caused a vibration which eventually became sound and this sound was Om. Om is the physical universe that corresponds to the original vibration that first arose at the time of creation. The Meditation is taught to inwardly transform this sound into the inner light which lights up ones thoughts and to bask in this blissful consciousness of light. Another way of saying Om is Aum. Aum is said to be the essence of all mantras and Vedas, the highest of all mantras or divine words:

"A"   Stands for Creation

"U"   Stands for Preservation

"M"   Stands for Destruction or Dissolution

This is the Trinity of God in the Hindu dharma (Brahma, Vishnu and Shiva). The three portions of the AUM relate to the stated of Walking, Dreaming and Deep Sleep. In the Vedas, AUM is the sound of the Sun, the sound of light. It is the sound of assent; it has the upward movement and uplifts the soul as the sound of the divine eagle and falcon.

2,000 years ago a Master Metaphysician named Jesus said; "We are the temple of God" that God dwells in us. Erick Butterworth in his book "Spiritual Economics" talks about the statement of Jesus being "The only begotten of God". Butterworth says we are all begotten of God. Jesus said "We are the temple of God" and "All these things I have done you can do also". In Science of Minds, we are expressions of God Manifest on this earth.

Jesus also said many times that "We are the Light of the world". "Let your light so shine before men, that they may see your good works, and glorify your Father which is in heaven." "While you have light, believe in the light, that you may be the children of light." "Ye are all the children of light." These Bible passages often were finished with instruction, that we must "Glorify the Father" or "Go to the Father" to have this light.

There are many philosophy references to us being "The Light of the World". My transformation didn't happen when I was saved as a child, or when I was baptized at the age of 12. I was baptized on November 2 and the ice of the creek was cracked to baptize us (I do remember that chilling experience). My transformation happened later in life with a change of my thoughts about God and my new interaction with God/Universe and my interdependence with God/Universe.

Earlier in my life I did it all myself. I didn't need help, didn't ask for help from anyone including God, until I messed up and needed God to fix something that I messed up. I feared this Anthropomorphic God and I thought he didn't like me much, so I did it my way. Even though I worked for the church, God was someone we talk about, like he was away or a relative we didn't like. This led to my breakdown of my life and leaving the church where God was supposed to be.

Then I embraced a new thought of God, a God that did not think or judge, but a God of the universe that wants to give to me, a God that empowers me to navigate my journey of life and to manifest my Dreams and Visions to my fullest potential. This is a God not to be feared but to be communicated with often. This God of the Universe wants me to have all the good that I want, including good situations, good work conditions and good of all kinds.

I began to change. I did not repelled people away from me because I was questioning myself, but my energy attracts people who want to be around because I've accepted who "I AM" and all my uniqueness. But what happened? I AM a manifestation of God/Universe on this planet! I began to talk daily with God/Universe and understand that right outside the skin of the Physical Temple God/Universe is everywhere and in everything. When I communicate and affirm what I want with God/Universe, the God/Universe outside of me starts the process of alignment. Things begin to happen, sometime slowly, sometimes quickly and things take different amounts of time depending on the amount of players God/Universe has to line up. God/Universe makes the "Path Straight" as the Advent scripture says; to set up for me, to do and be, as it is said, "GOD'S WILL". God's Will is for me to be the best Paul Campbell "I" can be.

I believe when I started trusting and became interactive with God/Universe as I am now, that a light in me started to shine. As Jesus said; "when you go to the Father, or Glorify the Father", then I make this connection; the light shines in me. We being God Manifest in human form is not enough. We must connect with all of God/Universe everywhere. It is why people now want to be with me, be around me, know who I am. Why does my music attract listeners? It's because it, through me, connects with God/Universe which is everywhere and is in everything that "I" do.

"I AM" Paul Campbell, an Individual Expression of God that is part of God/Universe. My talents and gifts were implanted at birth by God/Universe. It is now my responsibility to be the best I can be and let my light shine!

I AM the one and only
Paul Campbell
I Shine.

The Light which shines
In the eye
Is really the
Light of the heart

The Light which
Fills the heart
Is the
Light of God

Rumi

Four quotes that have helped me on my journey:

I ask not Oh Divine Providence for more riches, but more wisdom with which to accept and use wisely the Riches I received at birth, the power to direct and control my mind to whatever end "I" desire.

Napoleon Hill

Do not worry about anything; instead, pray about everything; tell God your needs and don't forget to thank God for his answer. If you do this, you will experience God's peace, which is far more wonderful than the human mind can understand.

Philippians 4: 6-7

What the Mind of Man can conceive and believe, it can achieve.

Napoleon Hill

Jesus said to him; "If you can believe, all things are possible to him that believes".

Mark 9: 23

Giving and Receiving:

The energy of God/Universe is a flow of energy, somewhat like a circle, flowing out from us and flowing back to us, we don't know when or where it will flow back from. Being a giving person is where our success begins, if we are always giving, we will always be receiving. Giving is first.

As you read the following pages and start to write, (script) Your Vision/Dreams and greatest goals, remember:

1. What do I want to achieve, what is my greatest goal?
2. How do I plan on giving back from my success?

And start giving NOW!

Your Vision Book
Thought, Word and Action

Your Vision, Your Dreams start as Thoughts

What you then think about
your Vision/Dream
Will determine
The Words you say about
your Vision/Dreams

Your Thoughts and Words
About your Vision/Dreams
Will determine your Action.

The Trinity of Metaphysics

Thought, Word and Action, is the Trinity of Metaphysical Manifestation. THE POWER of our Thoughts and Words drive the Action taken and determine what we receive on this journey, or if we allow anything to happen at all . . .

THOUGHTS: the energy and emotion that we place in our thoughts will determine what we create. If your thought is that "I'm not good enough", "someone else can do it but I can't", or "other people get the opportunities", what you are thinking will become true FOR YOU because of your thoughts. You will get very little opportunity, very little good, and probably not see the opportunity right in front of you <u>because you don't believe it can come to you.</u>

On the other hand, <u>if you know and believe that I am good enough</u> to do what I see in my mind, I can do as well or better than others, you will see a multitude of opportunities in front of you that others don't see. After we believe we can, we must have that Heart Energy, a Passion that drives our Vision/Dream.

WORDS: your Thoughts drive your Words, especially the spoken Word and what you put behind "I AM". The words you place after "I AM" will shape the direction of your journey. I often hear people say, "I'm not so and so", (and GOD/Source Energy responds, "you're not so and so"), "I'm not as good as so and so", (and GOD/Source Energy responds, "you're not as good as so and so"), "I can't do what others do", "who do you think I am", (and God/ Source Energy responds, "you can't do that"). If we believe as Jesus said (As by your belief), All things are possible, we either prophesy our Success or our Failure.

ACTION: once we believe in our mind and our heart that we can do it and say good things about what we are doing, GOD/Source Energy will give us opportunities when we take steps toward our Vision/Dreams. WE must take ACTION, take a class, write the article, practice our skill, and talk to others who have been successful in the field. Action must be taken and GOD/Source Energy will respond. GOD does not give us the Oak Tree, GOD gives us the seed to grow the tree. We must do the nurturing with GODS help. The Rev. Dr. Kennedy Shultz, founder of The Spiritual Living Center of Atlanta, GA said: "New life comes in to the world small and must grow, all GOD gives us is the opportunity (the seed) to grow into the Oak Tree". We must nurture the seed in us and when we do the most wonderful things happen, support flows from every direction.

And then, "We must thank GOD", not because God needs to be thanked, but because we need to be thankful.

Say Thank You
To
People;
Saying Thank you
Empowers them.

Say Thank You
To
God/Universe;
Saying Thank You
Empowers
You.

Out of Nothing, Out of No Way, A Way is Made.

Rev. Dr. Michael Beckwith

Too often we get caught-up in what part I am to play and what part God/Universe is to play in out Creating and Manifesting.

We forget to do what is at hand, to take the first step. Instead we try to do God/Universe's job and try to make things happen when we are not prepared. We often jump from "A" to "Z" without doing all the work and preparation in between. We are to take a firm first step, a firm second step, and God always opens doors, doors that did not exist will appear . . . Walk through them, continue taking steps and never stop expanding.

Taking a step is part of Action. There is another part of taking Action and that is, act as if it already exists. As a Pianist/Organist I practice every day, composing, keeping my skills at their highest. If there is a new place in music I wish to move into, I start leaning or composing music in that area, if there's a piece I want to play with someone, I learn it and the opportunity to play with them appears.

Preparing as if it is happening, is faith that it is happening. Jesus said: "Faith is the substance of things NOT SEEN, the evidence of things HOPES for".

In the last few years I have been Affirming and Scripting that I play more as a Pianist/Organist. I had primarily played in Protestant Churches over the years; I decided to expand in my thought to Catholic and Hebrew Services. Even though I have a Master in Sacred Music, I Still had some resistance to playing a Catholic Mass. My Affirmations worked, (as always) and I received several Opportunities to play Masses. I'm well educated, well prepared and always prepare the music for that particular service or Mass. I remember sitting at the organ console ready to play the Holy, Holy, Holy and wondering why I was still nervous about playing Mass? In a split second as I'm questioning myself, there was no reason for "Paul Campbell" Top Notch professional, educated, prepared to play this mass to still have this feeling . . . This feeling was from my past and in that split second I let go of that fear feeling from my past. To this day I am totally confident in playing a Mass. Change a thought, change my life.

We can affirm and things will show up but how we adapt will determine how much we accept into reality. The easier we adapt and let go of old thoughts the easier Good Flows to us. I also affirmed playing The Temple Hebrew Service; that opportunity came and I prepared and played with confidence. I'm continuing to grow, expand and learn more about the Hebrew Temple Service.

The flow of opportunities comes according to our being able to adapt and receive. Recently in a six day period I played 10 services, 6 Catholic Masses, 2 Hebrew Temple Services and 2 United Methodist Services. I was telling a Minster acquaintance about playing 10 services in six day and he said: "Wow, You're Lucky!" I thought, NO, I'm not Lucky, God/Universe does not gamble or play chance; it's an automatic.

Thought, Word Action and especially Action of Allowing, Action of Adapting, changing our thoughts on how it shows up. God/Universe, Source of all Good responds to us all the time.

Prentice Mulford, 19th Century Metaphysician wrote a paper in 1889 called, "Thoughts are Things". The last sentence of his 1889 paper says this:

> "There is no limit of the higher quality of thought they will accomplish who some will call Miracles. In this capacity of the human mind for drawing a thought current ever increasing fineness of quality of this power lies the secret of what some would call Magic."

Am I Lucky? NO, I live a Magical life provided by my connection and interdependence with God/Universe, Source of all Good.

I Live a Magical Life.
Out of Nothing,
Out of No Way,
A Way Is Made.

What's My Part?

Let me quote Bill Provost in his song, "Guess What?":

> Guess what I've got in my pocket, A pocket full of dreams.
>
> Guess what I feel in my heart, A heart full of love.
>
> Guess what I hear with my ears, An ear full of music.
>
> Guess what I see with my eyes, An eye full of beauty.
>
> And there's more than enough to go around; There's more than enough to go around; There are dreams for you; And dreams left over for the others too. Yes, there's more than enough to go around.

If we truly believe that God/Universe is All Abundant, All Wealth, All Substance, why do we suffer with the thought that there is not enough for me?

We have been taught, programmed and bullied by those who cannot manifest their own good. That is if they can't have their good, then you're not going to have your good. These people will usually spend their time investing in the control of someone else's life instead of creating their own life. In the 10 Commandments we are warned about this, it's called coveting. When we're coveting we are not creating and developing the gifts God/Universe gave each and every one of us; we are instead miss-directing creative energy.

How many times have we heard?
Who do you think you are?
Why can't you just fit in?
How do you think you are going to do that?

Believe in the great "I AM" in you and the unique gifts God/Universe has given you. Select a support person or group that you can vision with. Affirm that the Right and perfect visioning partner comes to you, and they will appear. Put into words with your visioning partner and support each other in taking the first step NOW.

Many are satisfied with the fantasy of creating
VS
Facing the illusion of FEAR to create

Face Everything and Rise
False Evidence Appearing Real
Forgetting
Everything's All Right

None of our Vision/Dreams and Gifts are the same; if we developed our UNIQUE GIFTS and contribute to the planet and mankind, Poverty would end.

Law of Attraction +
Law of Repelling –

I want to talk about this very popular thing called, "The Law of Attraction". "WE" do attract everything to us, out of our thoughts we create, whether we perceive it as good or bad . . . we attracted it. Most don't talk about the Whole Principle, The Law of Attraction is like a magnet, a magnet has two sides, The Attracting side + and The Repelling side –. There cannot be one side without the other side.

We cannot attract without letting go of things, stuff and Thoughts that no longer serve us. If we hold onto the old stuff, people, and especially Thoughts, the good will not come to us, or it may come to us and then be repelled away from us because we won't let go of what is stopping the good from flowing in.

The magnet has a Positive Side + and a Negative Side –, they have been miss labeled. The Positive Side has been labeled as GOOD and the Negative Side has been labeled as BAD. Both sides are GOOD. You cannot have one without the other. Failure and Success go hand in hand. Our failures are only an indicator of what we need to change or how we need to shift a bit to succeed. When we use our failure or things that didn't work out as we expected as an indicator and immediately shift our thoughts, The Repelling Side – becomes The Propelling Side. The Negative Side – is propelling us and the Positive Side + is attracting (pulling us forward), thus both sides are moving us in the same direction on our Journey.

After a while it gets easier to let go of stuff that is no longer useful; that stops the good from flowing in. BUT, the Law of Repelling can bite you in the ass, (that's a spiritual term). Depending on your motive, what is in your heart at the time of creating will determine what you receive. I have watched someone create an event or situation and because of what they were trying to prove, e.g. punish someone else, ("I'll show you", "don't get in my way") or create out of anger, the event didn't turn out as planned. All these motives are out of a low level attraction. The event will happen, but anybody who walks into the event with a higher vibration, (happy, smiling, with no agenda) will attract what you were trying to attract. You will repel and push to the people of higher vibration what you are wanting so badly.

This usually pisses off the person putting all their negative energy into creating the event. "IF" this person continues to create this way, (repelling what they are trying to create), they will continue to get the same results (repelling what they are trying to create). Soon they will create a Victim Mentality and soon believe that everybody is doing this to them, when they are attracting it to themselves and doing it to themselves. "The Law of Repelling —"always works.

I have attracted situations (often music playing positions) that are to be temporary on my journey. I'm there not to become permanent, but to teach and expand others and expand myself. Often I'm to meet a person who introduces me to another person of my vibration or common vision. The temporary situation is a stepping stone. When I'm repelled out of a temporary situation I ask for guidance on who am I to interact with to change the repelling into my propelling to the next situation? Often and most times the right and perfect person who likes what I do has already started talking to others to support and propel me forward to my next situation. How I leave a situation will determine what happens in the next situation. Bless and release.

Madea (Tyler Perry) said it best: Let people go . . . Some people come into our life for a lifetime and some come into our life for a season, don't mix up seasonal people with lifetime expectations. Seasonal people come into our life and teach us one thing and they are done. Let Then GO . . .

My take on it: Seasonal and temporary situations are not to be confused as a destination; they are part of the journey.

This is a wonderful journey for me, a learning experience. When I go to an event, party or anything with me happily loving myself, "I" usually, without trying, get phone numbers, book events for myself or am asked to do something on the spot at that event. "The Law of Attraction +" always works. I must know with discretion if it is appropriate for me to do what I'm being invited to do on the spot at someone else's event. Whether I say yes or no, out of respect of the situation, more opportunities will come on this journey. I have learned to allow.

Thank you God/Universe

Stream of Consciousness

Many years ago I started transforming my life; I started studying many philosophies, especially Science of Mind and Metaphysics. I was taught that everything that happens in my life I create, even the things that were not what I wanted. I started having a lot of guilt, because I had a vision of what I wanted and only part of it came, or it was not the quality that I wanted. I was punishing myself.

Then I was told a story. Creating a stream of consciousness (a stream of Manifesting) is somewhat like turning on a hose and putting the hose in the yard and allowing the water to flow down the side of the yard. At first, along with the water, comes a lot of dirt, grass and other particles; after a while the water gets clearer. The same happens when I start a stream of consciousness, many things and people feel the draw toward me and the stream flowing to me. Not all things that are attracted to me are of the quality that "I'm" desiring.

One day my computer went to a blue screen, OH NO, it crashed. I started to call my clients to say that we would have to use the phone instead of e-mail until I got a new computer. I decided to ask God/Universe for a new computer, in this process I told people that my computer had died and the flow of computers offered to me started.

Computer #1: Was offered by a woman who was very old and didn't have any consciousness of what a computer is. She said, "I have one in the closet at home that was my husband's, you can have it". She brought it to me in its beautiful leather case with a computer that was one of the first lap-tops. The screen was two inches square; the computer would not power up and had no way to connect to the internet. This computer was equal to her consciousness of life, out of touch with reality.

Computer # 2, 3 and 4: Three more computers were offered as loaners. Each had a different string attached. I said, "Thank You, No".

Computer # 5: I received a call from one of my adult piano students. He said to me, "Paul, do you know what I do for a living?" I said "no". He said, "I design computers for a company and I get computers given to me all the time; I have a new computer sitting here on the floor and you can have it". This computer was in perfect working order as the understanding of the givers consciousness. He knew what a computer is to be and it was a total gift.

Over the weeks that this played out, the stream of consciousness got clearer and clearer. "I" knew what I wanted, many people had a different idea of what a computer and giving is, from loans with strings attached to a total gift. Each computer was equal to the consciousness of the person offering or giving.

I'm not responsible for the givers consciousness, but I do get to say, "Thank You, No" and allow the stream of consciousness to continue until I receive what I desire.

Yes, I create with my thoughts, but I am just a part of it. I've become easier on myself when practicing creating and manifesting. Oh, and don't be afraid to say "Thank You, No" and then think to yourself "I" affirm something better.

The Rev. Dr. Kennedy Schultz, founder of the Spiritual Living Center of Atlanta said; "Nothing is too hard for God, and nothing is too good for me".

Above All

Think Good thoughts about yourself

Say Good things about yourself

Do Good things for yourself

Your Vision and Dreams
will Manifest faster

When you have

Begin Scripting
your NEW Life

The following pages are for you to get
started writing, (SCRIPTING)
Your Vision of your life, your dreams
Your GREATEST GOALS

1 Everything begins by saying GOOD things about
   yourself. "I AM beautiful", "I AM Generous". The
   first few pages have suggestions to get you started,
   after that it will just say: I AM_____,
   and you will have to affirm something GOOD about
   yourself.
2 When we learn to see God in the smallest things, the
   big things begin to happen. Everyday Script/Write
   "Thank You" for all the things that have already
   happened that day or yesterday.
3 If there is something that has not yet happened that
   is your plan, Affirm its existence, "The Way You See
   It". Write it out in detail; Act as if it's already here
   and prepare for it.
   Say "Thank You" to God/Universe, or whatever
   you call your source of energy.

Affirm its Existence

"Faith is the Substance of things not seen,
The evidence of things Hoped for"

Don't be afraid of asking for too
much or something too big,

ASK, AFFIRM and GIVE
THANKS for its existence

God doesn't need to be thanked
We need to be Thankful.

I AM **Successful**   Date_____

I AM *Abundant* Date_____

I AM **Good Looking**   Date_____

I AM **Happy**   Date_____

I AM **Prosperous**

Date_____

I AM *Loving*   Date_____

I AM *Giving*   Date_____

I AM **Rich**   Date_____

I AM **Calm**   Date_____

I AM _____   Date_____

I AM _____   Date_____

I AM _____   Date_____